Use this tried and tested strategy to

Fix Your Credit

Fast!

This course will help you to:

- Start your systematic recovery to credit worthiness in good time

- Rekindle your life ambitions

- Take full control of your finances

- Access loans, credit cards and mortgages in 12 months or less

- Reposition yourself for creative finance

- Be financially free!

- Apply same success principles in other areas of endeavour

Goodnews: you can improve your credit!

Content:

Modules	Titles	Page number
1	Our Guarantee	3
2	Get your credit analysis, *today*	11
3	Categories of entries on your credit file	29
4	Set the ball rolling: contact your creditors, *now*	40
5	Out of the red, into the green: move that credit score higher.	58
6	The power and place of F-O-C-U-S	65

Goodnews: you can improve your credit!

Module 1:
Our Guarantee

Congratulations for buying this course!

You have just made one of the best decisions in life ever; which is, to do something about your poor credit status. Rest assured that at the end of this course you will discover that your credit rating will become as great as you desire it to be and better than that, you would have picked up some success principles with which you can achieve success in any other area of your life.

That statement right there sounds bogus, unbelievable and perhaps unattainable. Well, that is expected because what you see on the cover is nothing new; in fact the internet is literally littered with several of such topics. However, this course is unique and result-oriented for the following reasons:

1) The principles and guideline outlined here have been tried and tested.
2) The course is presented in clear simple, concise and easy-to-follow steps.
3) The necessary information that you need to repair your bad credit are here in one place, you do not have to

---

Goodnews: you can improve your credit!

spend hours searching through hundreds of websites to find the info you need.
4) Sample letters have been drafted and included in word version for you to simply modify to suit your purpose.
5) The relevant addresses and websites that you may need, to check out certain information have been added as links, making each of them a click away.
6) The module on FOCUS, which is a synopsis of a different course, has been included here for you as bonus. The relevance of that module cannot be overemphasised. I would personally recommend that you read that module first, to get your motivation fired up from the start.
7) Lastly, you are guaranteed that if you will just follow the steps as they are laid out on this course, closely keeping to the time schedule, then no matter how bad your credit is at the moment, in just 12 months, your credit score will become so high that any high street lender will readily offer you credit facility for whatever purpose you desire. You can actually do this quicker.

This guarantee is based on the condition that you keep to your side of the bargain which is to read and sign this commitment page.

Goodnews: you can improve your credit!

I promise that:

1. I will complete this course,
2. I will stick to the time schedule,
3. I will follow every instruction on module 6,
4. When my credit rating starts to improve, I will carefully nurture it and will not ruin it by taking out credit cards or loans except for the purpose of repairing my credit even more,
5. When my credit rating reaches the point where I can conveniently take out credit facilities, I will only do so for investment purposes.

Your Full name: ....

Your signature: ....

You have automatically set yourself on the path of success because the only person that could have stopped you just made a promise to ensure you succeed. That person is you. So now, you're unstoppable!

Goodnews: you can improve your credit!

Going forward, it is important to understand that having low credit rating is not an accident; it is not a permanent condition either. It can go in either directions depending on your action or indifference. For those who face difficulties in reversing adverse credit rating, it is because they are inhibited by those impossibilities presented by their predicament, which is common to human.

Your decision to go by this book will however make your case an exception because this course gives you effective tools to demystify your ugly credit report and practically move you from red credit rating to green, at which point you would have internalised money-making skills. You do not need to pay a financial adviser; all you need is FOCUS.

Your time Schedule

Through experience and research, it has become clear that a time scale must be drafted and strictly adhered to if a set goal must be achieved within the given time. Therefore, I have put here a timetable that you will need to follow; to enable you stay focused and complete this course and achieve your results. This will help you shun distractions and stay focused.

Goodnews: you can improve your credit!

Section 1

> Day 1:
>
> 1) Take a plain sheet of paper and write boldly across: MY WHY.
>
> 2) Then write out all the reasons why you want to improve your credit rating.
>
> 3) Write out all the things you would be able to do, when your credit score becomes so high that you can easily access any amount of money you need.
> (It has to be a business, training/education, an investment etc; that would continue to generate more money for you)
>
> 4) Include the things that you would be able to do, if money was no longer an issue.
>
> 5) Read through module 6.

Section 2

> Day 2: -this section should take about 1-2 months to accomplish.
>
> 1) Read module 2 and apply for your credit report.
>
> 2) Then read module 3.
>
> 3) Read module 4 and use the guideline to put your income and expenditure together.
>
> 4) Use the sample letters to contact all your creditors accordingly.
>
> 5) If you work full time, I recon this whole process will take 1-2 months but could take less with some people though.

Goodnews: you can improve your credit!

Section 3

> This section of the process could take up to another
> 3- 6months
>
> 1) Read module 6 if you did not read it at the beginning.
> 2) Check your Vision board and your goal card, which of them have you accomplished and which of them are in the pipeline?
> 3) Your credit report should be looking better by now, no matter how little.
> 4) If you have to deal with difficult creditors, ensure you keep track of all your correspondence with them and no matter how much pressure there appears to be, do not give in to them. You must insist on your original offer of payment to each creditor. Remember to use the sample letters as they become relevant.
> 5) Read through module 5 and use the laid out guidelines on how to make one credit facility give you the benefit of 2.

Goodnews: you can improve your credit!

Section 4

This is the final section of the process and this should take roughly another 4-6months.

1) You should have noticed a huge improvement on your credit rating by now. So using the steps outlined in module 6, write out one of your major dreams that you really desire to accomplish

2) If you have successfully raised your credit rating in the last 6 months, then you can use the same method to begin to work on your dream

3) The barrier you had was not being able to access investments or life-improvement loans due to poor credit rating. As that has been resolved, you can now pursue your dream!

Goodnews: you can improve your credit!

Module 2:

Get your credit analysis today.

How did you get a bad credit?

The very first thing you must do today is to get your credit report. By that I mean go to www.noodle.co.uk (this is a *CallCredit* Agency); and fill in all your details including all the names you have been known by and all the addresses you have lived at in the UK.

Generally, people think they know the reasons why their credit rating got ruined but obtaining a credit report often springs up surprises. For example, unauthorized credit searches by companies against your name, CCJs (County Court Judgement) against you, by companies which you never obtained loans from or by companies which failed to follow proper procedures for getting the judgement. Others include settled accounts which still appear open on your file, fully settled or set-aside CCJs which appear active on your records. These are but a few of such possible surprises, so you must obtain your credit report without delay.

Goodnews: you can improve your credit!

It is important to mention here that if you have had a joint account or joint mortgage with someone in the past who ended up with an adverse credit, lenders may use that to judge your credit worthiness which could be the reason that ruined your credit rating.

All the reasons your credit rating became bad will be clear on your credit report so read through the document carefully. Once you identify the areas you disagree with, notify the credit agency immediately. There is an online query button beside every entry that leads you to a very short form which you can fill out on the agency's website. The agency will then investigate and if that information was put unto your records in error, it will be taken off immediately.

The Main UK credit Report agencies are:

1. *www.experian.co.uk*

2. *www.callcredit.co.uk*

3. *www.equifax.co.uk*

The different parts of a credit Report

The first time you obtain your credit report, it would look inundating. It would have so many pieces of information that discourages people from getting the full benefit of the report, so I will explain here the different aspects of the credit report and what they mean. Different agencies present these aspects differently, so for the purpose of clarity, I will use the outline of the credit report from noodle.

I) The Dashboard

When you log on to the website, your dashboard will open up. Here you will see the following:

- Your current credit score which is a number out of 700 (some other agencies score out of 1000). It will appear in a gauge-like graph.

- Your current credit rating from 1-5; 1 being very poor and 5, excellent.

- A scroll button to the right or left which will show the average credit score in your area and against the National average score.

- The number of searches against your name in the past 30 days.

- A total of your short term debt and long term debt

- The information stating how long till your next credit score.

- There will also be a display of certain credit cards and loans that you could possibly obtain, that is 'your matches'.

- Lastly, a green button that links you to your full credit report.

II) The credit report

This is the next page on your credit report file and here you will find the following:

- Personal Information

    This outlines your personal details, which include your full name; date of birth, current and previous addresses. Also, the date this record was created and the search reference number. There is also a piece of information asking you to contact them if you disagree with any of the information imputed there. At the end, there is a little advert about protecting your identity against identify fraud, this service comes at a price. It's a good thing but I recommend you concentrate on the job at hand for now which is improving your credit rating.

- The credit score

The next button is the "credit score". Here, the agency gives an explanation about your credit score for the current month and how it affects you. They also explain how and why your credit score is different from the score you may have been given by other credit agencies. Lenders do not base their final decision to lend you credit facility totally on your score; however, it is one of the criteria that many lenders use in the UK.

Generally, different lenders will put different things into consideration in giving you **a score** that will inform their final decision about your application. They will not show you this score but they are required by law, to let you know the particular agencies they have used in making that decision. The relevance of this is that you can then check if the agency provided the lender the correct information about you.

Goodnews: you can improve your credit!

In this section also, is a button the "noodle credit improve"; which leads to the page where they offer you a service for improving your credit rating, this also comes at a price.

Again, I recommend you ignore and rather work on it yourself first because a number of the things they are going to do, you can actually do yourself. Remember, you need every penny you can save for your debt repayment arrangement.

- Financial Account Information

Here is where the details of all your debts and repayments or defaults are outlined. It could span over several pages, depending on how many accounts you've had, how long you've had them for and how many payments or defaults have been entered against your name in those years. The defaults are marked in red and the up-to-date payments are marked in green.

Each of the accounts has a + button beside them that opens up when you click them to reveal the full details about the lender, the opening amount and the current balance, the last few digits of the reference number and your repayments or defaults. If you copy the name

---
Goodnews: you can improve your credit!

of the company unto 'Google', you can pull up their full contact details. All of the above information is true for all your open accounts. There is another button on this page that shows your closed accounts. Check through this list to ensure that all your settled accounts have been closed.

- Short term loans

This is the section where the credit agency shows details of any credit account information which they update more frequently. While you see the monthly update of your account, lenders see the daily updates. Lenders use this daily updates to make more timely and accurate assessments of your credit risk, potential fraud risks and whether you can afford the credit you've applied for. These accounts also appear in the financial account information section for up to 6 years but only stay in this section for 50 days.

- Search History

This section lists all the searches that have been made on your credit file through this particular credit agency in the last 24 months and they would stay on for 2 years. CallCredit (Noodle), does not use this as part of their criteria for giving you a credit score. However, many lenders include this as a criterion for offering you facility. So it is wise to limit, and if possible totally avoid any form of credit search against your name in the first 3 months of repairing your credit score.

- Address Links

This section details all the addresses linked with your financial activities. Meaning, a list of all your previous credit facilities and the address(es) you lived at whilst those credit facilities were active. Specifically, the source of the link is added here, the first confirmation and most recent confirmation are also added. Address link does not influence your credit rating with the credit agencies directly. However, if your name had been used for fraudulent purposes which you were not aware of, then this helps you uncover them and dispute them. For instance, if an ex-partner or a previous co-tenant who had access to your details, incurred debt on your behalf; this address link section would help you discover it. Disputing and reporting such acts would positively affect your credit rating.

- Connections and other names

In this section, the names of all the people linked with you financially are listed. For examples, joint loans, mortgages and the likes. If you were not aware of such loans, they could have adverse effect on your credit rating. There is this story about a couple who took out a joint loan but then parted ways without an agreement on how to clear the outstanding balance. A year after the split, the man moved to a different country. A couple of months after, the company tracked down the woman's UK address and began to chase her for the money. The woman explained that she had only co-signed the documents but never spent any part of the money. The company did not accept that excuse so the woman decided to just ignore the lender, hoping the issue would resolve itself somehow (some friends told her so).

But they were so wrong, because 2 years later, she found it impossible to secure a mortgage despite having enough money to pay a 30% deposit on the property. Unknown to her, that lender had obtained a CCJ against her for refusing to pay the loan. This is one

Goodnews: you can improve your credit!

of several hundreds of similar cases out there. So, finding out all addresses linked with your name is vital; to say the least.

To get yourself off this hook, you will need to write to the credit agencies that you are no longer in link with this person. They will update this on your file as long as the account is closed or loan paid off. However, there could be situations where neither has happened and **you really need to move on financially**, in that case, you must get in touch with the lender, explain your situation with as many proofs as you can find; and arrange a minimal repayment amount with them.

This is not a final solution but will get the account into green and reduce its impact on your financial status. Hopefully, you would be able to get the matter resolved with your ex; remember that the option of leaving it for much longer would drag you backwards.

If you have had accounts at your previous address such as store cards, old phone contracts which have ended or which you no longer use, thoroughly check that these have been closed. They can affect your credit rating if they stay active on your file. What I found in my case was that when I closed all my old accounts, my credit score went up the following month. While I strongly believe this as a part, and not the sole reason for increasing my credit score that month; taking the step is still most necessary.

Another list in this section is that of all the other names that you have used to obtain credit, for example if you had loans in your maiden name but now use your married name. So check that those loans are resolved and call the lender to inform them of your change of name. When I took out my first mortgage, it was in my maiden name. When I got married, I changed it with the lender and several years later when I checked my credit file, the original name I took out the mortgage in was no longer linked to my name because I had changed this with the lender.

- Electoral roll

This is another big issue that affects people's credit rating. What I found out in helping friends and relatives repair their bad credit was that nearly all of them knew that it was essential to get registered on the electoral roll to be able to get credit in the first instance.

However, they thought their details got automatically updated when they moved houses but this is not the case. When you move to a new address, you must update your details yourself; it takes less than 5 minutes to do. For people in England and Wales, the place to update your details is https://www.gov.uk/register-to-vote.

To repair your credit rating, you must do this because it is through the electoral register that lenders verify people's identity, which means if you cannot be identified as one who lives at where you claim to live, then you're a fraud, it's rude but it's true. For one thing, remember that the lenders that you wish to obtain credit from, take a huge precaution to be sure that the person they are dealing with is not a fraud, so any name which cannot be checked on the electoral roll, stands no chance at all. So do this like; this minute; if you haven't done so.

- Public Information

This is the section where details of any Court judgements, Insolvencies, Bankruptcies in your name are listed. Generally speaking, insolvencies refer to agreements between yourself and your lenders to pay off your debt. Things like IVA or personal debt repayments plans fall into this category. There are clear legal steps to follow before becoming insolvent. My advice is this: if you have any debt repayment arrangements in place, keep up with your payments and clear them off. They stay on your records for up to 6 years and they have an impact on your credit-worthiness with lenders. However, as I have emphasised here severally, there are many ways to make you become credit worthy again. So, while waiting to clear off such items from your credit file, you can begin putting to practise the information presented here and you will become credit worthy in a very short while. The greatest danger here is refusing to do something about the situation but buying this course and taking the steps prescribed here; you have taken yourself off that danger zone.

- Notices of correction

When you raise a dispute, the credit agency will investigate it and if that leads to a correction then such information are listed in this section. Also, all the statements which you have requested to be added to your file about certain items which are "true" but have the potential to present a misleading picture of your credit status to lenders; are also included here. To be specific, if you had gone into default on your mortgage for instance but can show that it was due to a legitimate factor such as illness or accidents which incapacitated you, sudden loss of a job and the like. These statements will be added to your file even if it's not obvious how this would improve your credit rating; it will surely put you in a better light with lenders. Since lenders have varied ways and criteria for deciding who to lend to, this could be a positive indication rather than not. So, such statements, if necessary; are worth the trouble.

- CIFAS

This stands for **Credit Industry Fraud Avoidance System**; this is the section that shows if your name has been linked with any form of fraudulent activity of some sort. Often, people who become victims of identity theft or fraudsters realise this a little too late; because by the time they discover this, they would have suffered great financial setback, resulting in adverse credit rating.

I strongly believe that one of the greatest benefits of obtaining a credit report is the fact that you can find out if your identity or documentation have been used fraudulently. Identity theft is an area of huge concern for the Governments of all Nations and should be for you. More importantly, all lenders check such fraud record registers before they make a decision to give you credit facility. It is worthy of note that some insurance companies may register a fraud against your name if you had been found wanting in making an insurance claim or presenting false documentation in order to obtain cheaper insurance premium. If this happens, you must write to the company that holds this against you to find out their reasons and then follow through with their procedure for redressing and removing this from your file. If you disagree with this and have proof, then raise this with the organisation. If they fail to deal with it properly and promptly, you can write to the costumer complains ombudsman (address provided in the glossary).

Goodnews: you can improve your credit!

The above are the most important aspects which can impact your credit rating. However, other sections include:

III) Noddle Extras

> This is the section where this credit agency advertises how they can help you rebuild your credit rating, improve it if it's not that bad and how they can help you protect your identity and things like that. ...Great offers, but at a price. ...So, my advice? Don't take any of them, because you can DIY- Do-it-yourself.

IV) Card matcher

> On this page, you can fill out a quick form that will then do one search to find all the cards that you could obtain considering your financial status. In my case, I remember that when I first pulled up my credit report and did this, no offers came up but within three months of working on my credit records, 5 offers came up. This is a good sign.

Goodnews: you can improve your credit!

V) Loan matchers

Here you can fill out a quick form that will then bring up loan companies that would lend you some money, and the likelihood of that happening is shown and explained beside each company. However, as you are trying to rebuild your credit rating, applying for loans is not just an option yet.

VI) Utilities

Here you get the opportunity to compare phone, broadband, electricity/gas and TV companies. If you have been with the same provider for ever, then I suggest that you try this utilities compare system.

You could save yourself several hundred pounds yearly by switching your service provider. In my case, through this section, I was able to save £150 on my gas and electricity bill for one year. This made me to also do the same thing with my car insurance. Rather than renew with my then provider, I shopped around and saved a whopping £500 on my renewal quote. These savings were money that I desperately needed because if I had been saving like that in the years gone by, I would have managed my finances better and not end up with such a poor credit rating. So the benefits of taking steps to repair your credit score cannot be overemphasised.

Goodnews: you can improve your credit!

Module 3:

Categories of Entries on your Credit file

The types of entries you may find on your credit report include **soft** or **hard** quotation footprints. Certain searches can be done against you when insurance companies make quotes for insurance for you. They are called soft searches and should not affect your ability to get credit. Although, if you searched for yearly paid car insurance offers, they will do a hard search which will affect your credit score and stay on your file for 2 years. My advice would be to do a search for insurance that are monthly paid because you can always make a yearly payment for the quote that you decide to take.

If you want soft footprints removed from your report, you can contact the insurance companies directly and they will remove them. In my own case, I had to remove all such footprints against my name; soft or hard; because my credit rating was so terrible that anything removable was well worth it. Also, I found out that after removing these entries, I a credit card company pre-approved me for a credit card, although at an unbelievably high APR. I obviously turned it down but it was my first sign that my credit rating was beginning to improve.

Goodnews: you can improve your credit!

A **soft footprint** stays on your file but it's not visible to future lenders, and it does not affect your credit rating. The **hard footprint** on the other hand, takes off about 10% of your credit score, and lenders can see it. So this is the one that does the 'damage' to one's credit rating. Each hard footprint stays on your file for 2 years and then it gets dropped off. Although it could generally affect your rating for 12 months, according to FICO; it is the first 6 months that affects you the most. FICO is an acronym for Fair Isaac Corporation, the name of the company which created it. Basically, "**FICO score** is a type of **credit score** that makes up a substantial portion of the **credit** report that lenders use to assess an applicant's **credit** risk and consider whether to extend a loan or not".

Another type of entry which adversely affects your credit rating is County Court Judgment (CCJ). *(First of all, CCJs can be avoided and I have a very short and cheap course on how to avoid getting CCJs in the first place.)* You must query any CCJ you do not recognise and you can also remove genuine ones from your records. To do this, you will need to write a letter to all your creditors, offering them an amount to clear the balance with the condition that they would **set aside** the order or judgement. For lenders to accept your offer, you will need to fill out an income and expenditure form. (The step by step guide to doing this and a sample form is in the next module.

Other entries are *repossession* and *bankruptcy*. These will stay on your records for a total of 7 years for repossession, 7 years for chapter 13 bankruptcy and 10 years for chapter 7 bankruptcy. Chapter 7 bankruptcy by definition;

> "...is a liquidation proceeding in which the **debtor's** non-exempt assets, if any, are sold by the **Chapter 7 trustee** and the proceeds distributed to creditors according to the priorities established in the Code.. Chapter 13 bankruptcy is also called a wage earners plan.
>
> It enables individuals with regular income to develop a plan to repay all or part of their debts. Under this **chapter**, debtors propose a repayment plan to make instalments to creditors over three to five years." - quizlet.com

Another is the IVA (Individual Voluntary Arrangements) which stays on your record for 6 years, meaning that if an IVA is arranged for a period of 5 years, it can only be seen for a further 12 months after it has been settled.

Goodnews: you can improve your credit!

There is nothing you can do about these entries staying on your credit file for these numbers of years, nevertheless, at the end of this course, you would have received the tools to begin to rebuild your credit file and having access to loans and credit for the business and investment purposes/goals you've set for yourself. If obtaining a mortgage is one of such pursuits of yours, we can give you an overview on how to buy houses without mortgages or any of your money in. For that, send us an email and we will sign post you accordingly.

None of these entries on your file?

If you do not have any of the above on your file yet, then your case is easier and it's quicker to get your credit file on track. Our advice here would be that you make a private arrangement of repayment with all your creditors. In rebuilding my credit, I found out that creditors that had stopped chasing me for money suddenly began chasing me as soon as I made a repayment arrangement with the others. So in calculating your income and expenditure; include all of the debts that you owe. It is important to know that every default entered on your file, stays there and visible to lenders for a period of 6 years. Even when you have settled it, it would stay there for the 6 years from the date of the default.

Despite this fact, it is still possible to get your credit rating on the upward motion if you take the right steps. For instance, if there was a genuine reason for the default such as ill health, the loss of a job, accident or the like, then you can write a note to the credit report agency and they will put it on your file. This is called a 'notice of correction' (NOC). NOCs do not automatically increase your credit rating but they put you in a better standing with lenders; and once a lender lends you credit, another one will and another will. If you take these credits and begin to manage them as you should, then your credit rating will begin to sky-rocket.

The contact addresses and phone numbers of all your creditors are usually listed on your credit report. If for any reason, they are not listed, it could mean the debt may have been sold off to a different recovery company.

So, you must Google the original lender's address, write them about the debt and they will send you the company that currently manages that particular debt.

Goodnews: you can improve your credit!

CCJs are avoidable

A creditor has the right to obtain a CCJ against you if you fail to pay off the amount you owe them. CCJs are very serious legal indictments which affect your ability to obtain any form of credit such as phone contract, bank accounts, and certain forms of insurance, credit cards, store cards, loans, mortgages or even delayed payment plans in stores. Not having access to such facilities for a period of 6 years can be a pain to say the least. You must take the warnings of these companies seriously. To avoid getting CCJs, there are few things you can do:

1) Do not Ignore

Usually, when people start receiving letters from their creditors; they take the 'easy' way out, ignore them. This unfortunately turns out to be the hardest route. So, you must never ignore but stay in regular contact with your creditors; even if that means explaining the reason why you are unable to make payments. A number of lenders would allow you about 30 to 60 days to sort things out. To be quite honest, I found out that some will even extent the period for a further 30 days if you are making some effort to seek help, for instance if you are temporarily jobless and have then signed on to JSA (Job Seekers Allowance) and can show evidence that you are actively searching for jobs. This would have given you a good 3 months to find a way to avoid getting a CCJ.

2) Seek Professional Help

You will need to visit your local Citizens Advice Bureaux (CAB) for a free financial assessment. Sometimes, there are ways that you can get help with managing your debts that you are totally unaware off. Also, this professional help which is completely free, will give you a great overview of how to go about settling your debts and also how to avoid increasing them; by that I mean how to avoid loan sharks who promise to solve your debt problem if you take out a one for all loan with them. These companies are terrible, so avoid them like a plague. The greatest thing about the CAB is that if your case falls outside of their jurisdiction, then they will adequately signpost you.

You can easily pull up your local CAB on Google and if you do not have access to the internet, you can use the free one in your local Library or your local county council office.

Goodnews: you can improve your credit!

3) Pay it off or set aside

Generally, you can avoid the CCJ by paying off the entire amount owed in 30days. If however, you couldn't pay within 30 days, there is still a benefit to paying off the full amount on time. Once you have paid in full, you could send the evidence of your payment and financial status to the credit agency that would put a note of "satisfied" beside this CCJ on your file. Although the CCJ is held on your credit file for 6 years from the date the plaintiff won it, a note of "satisfied" would be placed beside it.

This information is available to lenders and can positively influence their decision to grant you loan. After the CCJ has been issued, you can request the court to set it aside. This can be really difficult because the instances of success are very slim but possible.

The grounds for requesting a CCJ set aside are:

- If the process was wrong. That is, if the company did not follow through with the guideline for filling for CCJ against a person. This guideline is available from this website: https://www.gov.uk/county-court-judgments-ccj-for-debt/overview

- If you didn't receive the letters of court hearing (you must attend all court hearings to make an offer of repayment); don't bury your head in the sand about your debt.

- If you lost your job or were ill or you didn't owe the money in this first place. The CCJ's will be set aside but be careful, the case might be heard again and if you are found liable, you will end up with a CCJ over a longer period because the process will start all over again.

  Also, this will cost you £75 and a lot more or even a sentence if you did not have a cogent reason for requesting a set aside order. As this would mean a resubmission by the creditor, it means that if granted in the end, the time that CCJ stays on your records would be a lot longer. So you must be very clear and seek professional advice before you go down this route.

4) You could get a CCJ removed

...from your file if the plaintiff was an insurance company. If you contact the credit agency with the

Insurance Company's letter that shows the case number of the judgement, the date and amount; the agency will remove it from your file. All that said, let me reiterate that in repairing your bad credit, paying off the debt for which you got the CCJ is the safest way to go.

5) Other things you could do

If you cannot avoid getting a CCJ in the first instance, there is little that you can do than to pay it off. In nearly all of the times, the agency collecting the debt would agree to a repayment as small as £1 per week depending on your circumstance. Once you have this in place and maintain that repayment, the effect of this CCJ can be greatly reduced. If you are repairing your credit rating, then you want to take all your payments, CCJs and other forms of defaults, from red to green, so an arrangement to pay off is your first option.

In some cases, it could be that the CCJ had been issued in error, and then you can make a counter claim to have the court reverse the order.

You do this by writing to the court with all the evidence you have. Once the court upholds your counterclaim, the credit agency will be notified and they will amend this on your file within a few weeks. Whatever you decide to do about your CCJs, please seek professional help because the chances that the CCJ(s) have been issued in error are so slim that it is almost impossible to remove them. Once one has been registered against you, it will stay on your records for the duration of 6 years and drop off automatically.

Module 4:

Contact your Creditors today

How to find your creditors' contacts

Take a note pad and list all the entries which are marked red on your report (all your defaults that is). Include their full details (addresses and contact numbers) you can find this outlined on your full report. I have found out that different agencies use different methods to enter your creditors' contacts, so check carefully. I also found out that some may not list all of them while some pick and choose the ones to list. So I strongly recommend that you obtain your report from the 3 agencies I listed in module 1. That way, you will have nearly all the contacts, if not all, you need.

When you contact these agencies, some will not respond, some will write to say the account is no longer with their company and will give you the creditor they passed it over to. Or, you can contact the original lender, quoting the original reference number, and they will send you the name of the current company that has the account.

Goodnews: you can improve your credit!

A number of them(especially the ones who put the "red" default notice on it each month) would be sending letters to you in the post anyway.

How to fill out the Income/Expenditure Form

With your contact list done, you're ready to set out your repayment plan, so at this point, you will fill out the form. A number of people find this a chore and they give up here but you won't because I have made it *bread and butter* for you. So, kindly log on and pull up one of such forms from any of the following websites:

- ✓ https://www.moneyadviceservice.org.uk/en/tools/budget-planner
- ✓ www.nationaldebtline.org
- ✓ https://www.citizensadvice.org.uk/debt-and-money/budgeting/budgeting/work-out-your-budget/

You have to ensure that at the end of this form, you have a total of £100-150 to service these loans monthly. If you are unemployed, then you can request via email for a free copy of an e-leaflet, *"5 quick steps to making mega-money starting at £0"* which I can give as a bonus.

Goodnews: you can improve your credit!

Handy tips for filling out the form

1. Ensure you use a form with an online calculator, that is, that automatically calculates as you go along

2. Most of these forms cannot be saved online so you must print it off once you're done, but if you are allowed to save it then please save as you go along.

3. Fill in all your income. This includes wages from paid employment, all the benefits you receive, pensions, income from self-employment and any money you receive on a regular basis, say from a partner or the like. If you are married or live with young adults who work or receive benefits, you will need to do this as a household income. That is, all the money that comes into the house, monthly or weekly. You choose weekly or monthly and keep this the same all through the form.

4. Next will be your priority out-goings or spending such as your rent/mortgage, electric and gas bill, water rate, TV licence, child maintenance pay, child care cost, service charge or ground rent, fuel, hire purchase payments e.g. for car, council tax, County Court Judgement and other fines.

Goodnews: you can improve your credit!

5. Then your other spending will need to go on the form. You have to be careful here because if you put an amount that is unreasonable or frivolous, the lender may reject your offer of payment. On the debt helpline website, if you click the question mark beside each column of the form, a brief explanation is provided which guides you on acceptable amounts for each spending. But just to name a few are things like; your insurances, transport, alcohol/cigarettes, church contributions, road tax, household appliance rental, breakdown cover, accidents and emergency cover, education fees, telephone costs, cable and internet subscriptions etc

6. Your living cost will include food, prescriptions, laundry, toiletries, clothing, petrol, dentist, sports (e.g. gym membership), parking etc. This is a general guide and covers nearly all areas.

7. The next thing is to fill out all your debts. The priority debts are usually separated from the other debts. Priority debts are debts like mortgages, secured loans (taken out against your mortgage- if these are not paid, your property will be repossessed),

---

Goodnews: you can improve your credit!

Council tax debts, Court fines, traffic fines. These are debts which could lead to prosecution, so they are called priority debts.

Non-priority debts are pay day loans, credit cards, store cards, gas and electric bills, water rates and the like. The fact that they are referred to as non-priority debts does not make them have less effect on your credit rating. So I'll say this is just for the purpose of classification, every debt must be given proper consideration in getting your credit repaired.

8. After you have done the form, save a copy and print a copy off. If you can't print it immediately, then use your mobile phone to take a picture of it or email a copy to yourself.

Completing the Table

Now that your form is filled out, you're ready to do some mathematics! To do that, you will need a table like the one below:

Company	Reference Numbers *	Debt (£)	Amount offered (£)
A	AXZ12077	1,109	10.50
B		4,198	39.70
C		2,780	26.30
D		300	2.80
E**		660	6.20
F		780	7.30
G		200	1.90
H		132	1.20
I		109	1.00
J		298	2.80
TOTAL Debt		10,566	99.70

Goodnews: you can improve your credit!

Calculation: amount owed/total owed X £100

So, using the company we have called A, it would be 1,109 divided by 10,566 equals =0.1045 multiplied by 100, equals =10.49. You can round this up to **£10.50,** and that's the amount that you will offer to company "A". The greater your debt, the higher the total amount you should set aside for repayment. At the end of all calculations, you will discover that all the repayment amounts offered to your creditors equal £100 or just under. After this, write a letter to each of your creditors with the offer of payments. Below is a sample that you could use to quickly get yours done.

<u>Sample Letter 1</u>

Now you will need to write a letter to each of your creditors with the offer of payment laid out on the table above. You will need to add a copy of your income and expenditure form and a copy of the table to show that it is a fair offer of payment that you are making them. On this offer of payment, it is important to ask them to freeze further interests on this account.

The main reason experts advise against using a debt management company is to save you money and for the fact that there is nothing they could do about your debts that you couldn't do yourself.

Goodnews: you can improve your credit!

112 Oxford Drive

Ipswich

IP44 9VF

22 March 2016

The Manager,

Abbey Union Debt Recovery

Unit 57,

109-110 Abington Crescent

London SE8 7AG

Dear Sir,

REFERENCE NUMBER: ZP/11097 **

I write regarding the above debt which I originally owed to Halifax Bank which you currently manage. I hereby make an offer of £6.20 monthly to clear off the balance. If this is acceptable to you, kindly send me details of your bank account so that I can set up a standing order to have that money paid to you on the 10th of each month with effect from the 10th of April, 2016.

Goodnews: you can improve your credit!

I hereby request that you freeze all further interests on this account and if you cannot freeze the interest, kindly write and let me know your reasons.

Yours Truly,

Mrs Ida Augustus

What if my creditor refuses my offer?

When you send these letters out to your creditors, some will accept and others will refuse. Some might accept but refuse to freeze interests. Even if they refuse to accept or freeze interests, you must begin making the offered payments to the creditors. Their bank details can be found on the letter that they had sent to you but if not, you can call each of your creditors and request their bank details before you send out the letters. Then you write them after the refusal. Here is a sample to use for your second letter.

Goodnews: you can improve your credit!

Sample letter 2

112 Oxford Drive

Ipswich

IP44 9VF

30 March 2016

The Manager,

Abbey Union Debt Recovery

Unit 57,

109-110 Abington Crescent

London SE8 7AG

Dear Sir,

REFERENCE NUMBER: ZP/11097 **

I write regarding your reply to my letter dated 22 March 2016 in which you refused to accept my offer of repayment.

Please, I would like to re-explain to you that in my present financial circumstance, I am unable to pay any amount more than £6.20. This is because many of my other creditors have

Goodnews: you can improve your credit!

accepted the offer of payment which I have begun to pay to them. If I was to increase your payment, then I will not be able to keep up with all my payments which will keep me longer in debt. You have my assurance that I will increase this payment to you if my circumstances improve in the future.

Please note that I have begun making my proposed offer to you as a goodwill gesture. I am really prepared to resolve this account, so kindly accept my offer of £6.20 monthly.

Also, find attached to this letter, a table of analysis of all my creditors with their offer of payments, a copy of my income and expenditure form and copies of acceptance letters from 2 of my other creditors.

Yours truly,

Mrs Ida Augustus

If they still refuse after this letter, write them a 3rd letter using the sample letter 3 below:

Sample Letter 3

112 Oxford Drive

Ipswich

IP44 9VF

22 April, 2016

The Manager,

Abbey Union Debt Recovery

Unit 57,

109-110 Abington Crescent

London SE8 7AG

Dear Sir,

REFERENCE NUMBER: ZP/11097 **

I write regarding my first 2 letters to you and your subsequent refusal to accept my offer of repayment. I have explained to you the reasons why I will not be able to increase my offer of

---

Goodnews: you can improve your credit!

repayment to you in my first 2 letters while I have carried on making the offer of payment.

Your persistent refusal to accept my offer of payment or to freeze further interests have left me with no other choice than to write a letter of complaints to your company's complaints department. Therefore, could you kindly send me the contact details of that department please?

Yours truly

Mrs Ida Augustus

At this point 99% of companies would accept your offer of repayment or pass the debt unto a different debt collector agency. All you need do is to send them the first letter you had sent to this company, remember to put the address of the new agency and the new date. But if they refused then it will be time to send a letter to the company's complaints team, using the sample letter below:

Goodnews: you can improve your credit!

Sample letter 4

112 Oxford Drive

Ipswich

IP44 9VF

3 May 2016

The Manager,

Abbey Union Debt Recovery

Unit 57,

109-110 Abington Crescent

London SE8 7AG

Dear Sir,

REFERENCE NUMBER: ZP/11097 **

I hereby write this letter to complain about the way and manner your company has persistently refused to accept my offer to clear off the debt that I owe. Please find attached copies of my correspondence as well as the replies of refusal that I have received.

Goodnews: you can improve your credit!

Could you kindly look into this matter and reconsider your position because I am not able to increase my offer of repayment in my present financial condition. Please note that I have carried on making the offer of payment since the month of March 2017.

Yours truly

Mrs Ida Augustus

At this point, it will be glaring that you are not ready to shift grounds, so the company will either accept your offer or pass on the debt to a different company in which case you will send the very first letter to this new debt collections company.

But if they still refuse at this stage, you must send a letter to the financial Ombudsman Service via email, complaint.info@financial-ombudsman.org.uk or write them through the post using this address:

The Financial Ombudsman Service

Exchange Tower

London E14 9SR

Goodnews: you can improve your credit!

I will highly recommend that all of these letters to the companies are sent through emails, this would help you save on the cost of postage. Remember that there is free internet Wi-Fi at the local libraries across England and Wales.

You can use the sample letter below:

Sample Letter 5

>112 Oxford Drive
>
>Ipswich
>
>IP44 9VF
>
>**3 June 2016**

The Manager,

Abbey Union Debt Recovery

Unit 57,

109-110 Abington Crescent

London SE8 7AG

Dear Sir,

REFERENCE NUMBER: ZP/11097 **

I write to complain about the way and manner (name of company) has refused to accept my offer of repayment despite several letters to them and a letter of complaint to the company's complaints department.

Could you kindly look into this matter on my behalf please? Please be informed that since I made the offer of repayment, I have carried on making the payments and I believe that I have taken all the necessary steps towards resolving this issue with the company, all to no avail.

Kindly find attached copies of my correspondence with this company till date.

I will be most obliged if my request is granted and this matter resolved accordingly.

Yours truly,

Mrs Ida Augustus

No doubt, this process seems winding and tiring, which is why so many people don't bother, but the benefits are so enormous that you can't quit! As a way of keeping your motivation up, go back and check your credit file, the progress you would have made since you began this journey are bound to spur you on.

> *"Continuous effort, not strength nor intelligence; is the key to locking our potential."* -Winston Churchill

In my experience and in helping friends and family members; only a few creditors allow things to get to this extent. In one of my cases, the court ended up asking the creditor to hold off chasing me for the debt for 2 years and that after the 2 year period, they should re-access my financial status to ascertain if I could begin making payments. Needless to say that I never heard from that company again and the loan never reflected on my credit file.

Goodnews: you can improve your credit!

Module 5:

Out of the red, into the green, time to push that credit score higher!

Using the above sample letters and following the rules discussed in the preceding module, will definitely set you on the road to raising your credit score to the highest level possible. To speed things up, you need to take this vital step. Obtain a credit-repair credit card. These are mainly prepaid and do not require credit cheques to be approved. Once you receive your card, you can preload with cash without being charged a fee or interest when you spend your money but at the same time, the transactions will be recorded against you as though you were using an actual credit card, thus improving your credit score. Other benefits of these cards are:

- ✓ interest free top-up,
- ✓ Accepted anywhere you see the MasterCard sign, online, in stores, over the phone and in over 200 countries of the world.

- ✓ Can act as a bank account because you can have your wages paid into it and set up direct debits from it
- ✓ You can obtain overdraft facility up to £100 interest-free for up to 12 months
- ✓ The overdraft limit can be up to £250

Examples of such credit cards and where they can be found include:

1. POCKIT (card fee -£0.99)
   http://www.pockit.com/affiliates/money?utm_source=money&utm_medium=affiliate&utm_campaign=standard

2. CASHPLUS (card fee -£5.99 then £9.99 monthly)

http://www.mycashplus.co.uk/offers/cashplus/tabs/deluxeod.aspx?pc=MUK852

3. The i-account (card fee -£4.95, then £9.95 monthly)

   https://secure.membersaccounts.com/OnlineApp/Page1.aspx?pc=CLR015&ref=http://icount.co.uk/&tn=CPCLEARCASH

Goodnews: you can improve your credit!

These 3 are some that I would personally recommend, here are so many others from the credit card compare website and they all have very similar terms and conditions.

A serious Warning here please:

> "Manage your credit card well, especially the overdraft facility!"

Getting your credit back on track is a very serious business and as such, you must be very careful how you manage this card especially when you get to the point where the card company agrees to grant you an overdraft facility. To help you achieve this proper management, do the following:

- ✓ Open a separate bank account and apply for a credit card. Let's refer to this separate account as "The repair Account".

- ✓ Set aside a sum; say £200 in the repair account. This will be the money; the "catalyst" that will speed up the rate of your credit repair process.

- ✓ When you receive your card from these credit card companies ensure you sign it and activate it immediately.

- ✓ Then use this card for your normal household essentials like bread, milk, toiletries and the likes, spend about one third of the total limit.

- ✓ Then as soon as you receive the statement, transfer the full balance from the repair account into your credit card account.

- ✓ Then top up the repair account again to £200.

- ✓ Repeat the process all over again.

After doing this for 3 months, go back and check your credit rating. I can guarantee that you would have at least improved it to a reasonable margin of say 10-20% at the minimum. Apart from that, you will notice that about 6 credit card companies would be offering you credit facility. This will be shown on your credit report profile, in the section marked "your offers".

At this point, I will highly recommend that you take one of the offers from a high street bank. Once this has been approved, your credit problem is nearly over! Because for one thing, this financial organisation of high repute is giving you money that is not yours to spend, meaning you are credit-worthy again.

Goodnews: you can improve your credit!

But the battle is not won yet, so you must set aside a higher amount of money in the repair account. Then use your new credit card for shopping and pay off the balance as you are now in the habit of doing. If you were to carry on doing this for another 3 months, a loan company will be willing to offer you loan. My candid advice: DO NOT TAKE IT! The APRs are over the roof and not worth the trouble at all.

As you carry on for the next 3 months, bringing you to your 9th –month-point of this journey, you will find that the high street banks will be offering you credit facilities like loans and even mortgages, provided other criteria are satisfied. At this point, your credit score would have reached about 40-60% of the credit agency's highest score.

Now, you have to carefully look at the offers each bank is making you and go with the one that offers 0% interest rates. They will all have APRs but go for the one that gives you say interest free on purchases for like the first 6 months. Use this credit facility and PAY off the total balance each month. This way, you incur 0% or very minimal interest on using this OPP (Other Peoples' Money).

Goodnews: you can improve your credit!

BOGOF your credit repair speed

You can *BOGOF* the rate at which you are improving your credit score. By BOGOF, I mean buy-one-get-one-free on these credit facilities. Let me explain: Once you're able to get high amounts of credit facilities from the normal high street banks, you will be able to double the rate at which you're improving your credit rating. Say for example if you get a credit card from Barclays for £1,000 at 0% interest. You can use this credit card to buy a bed or sofa or the like from a shop like Argos for instance, that will offer you a 3 month interest free payment plan. So, in the first month that you purchase your goods, you pay nothing, rather, you set aside the money that you would have paid at the time of purchase in the repair account.

Then in the second month, you pay 80% of the cost of the goods from your credit card. As soon as you receive the statement of the credit card, you pay it off using the funds from the repair account.

Goodnews: you can improve your credit!

Then in the third month, you pay off the balance 20% using your credit card again. Now, Argos will be so pleased with you that they will offer you their store card (you're becoming even more credit worthy). Then from the repair account, you pay off the entire credit card balance; repeat the process if needs be.

The relevance here is that if you had paid for your goods directly, nothing would have happened to your credit rating. But by simply moving money around in this manner, you would have built reputation with 2 well established lending houses. This will greatly shoot up your credit score. By the end of 12 months, your credit rating would have been so good that any lender would be willing to offer you credit facility including loans and mortgages at the best APR possible.

Goodnews: you can improve your credit!

Module 6:

The Power and place of FOCUS

How soon do you want to get your credit totally clean? How quickly do you want to be completely debt-free and gain your financial freedom? Well, it's possible if you can just focus. Yes, F-O-C-U-S! Meaning:

- F –Forget the past
- O –Open your mind to its endless possibilities
- C –Create a vision board
- U –unleash your potentials within and
- S success will be inevitable

F- Forget the past

"The secret of change is to focus all of your energy, not on fighting the old,
but on building the new"
-SOCRATES

So many people spend their lives looking behind; they allow the failures of yester-years ruin the glorious chances today offers; for building a happier, brighter, healthier and wealthier tomorrow. But if you could just take a look around you, you would quickly see that the world you live in is full of endless opportunities. And as the Bible implies; the reason every body's life is divided into 'starts' and 'stops' (day and night), is so we can each have a brand new opportunity to make success of the *now,* despite the shortfalls of the past because success is never final and failure, never fatal (Winston Churchill).

So, you must deliberately, consciously; forget the past (stop obsessing about it). For the state you are in today, does not define who you are, but *who you were.* In other words, the 'you' you see today is the outcome of the predominant thoughts you held about you before today. "Thoughts become things" (Napoleon Hill), so if you want a new *you* tomorrow, think new thoughts today. Think new thoughts by following these steps:

1. Take a clean sheet of paper and write down the success that you desire. This could be anything. Write it down in clear terms and in great detail. Is it money you

Goodnews: you can improve your credit!

desire? How much? Write it down. Or do you need happiness, better relationships or improved health?

2. Do you want a credit score that will enable you access the finances you need for a business? Become a very successful entrepreneur? Then write in down. Remember, 'a goal not written is just a wish' (Steve Maraboli). So turn your wishes into goals by writing them down and then setting a specific date for its realisation. Don't worry about how it will happen, for "goals are like magnets. They'll attract the things that'll make them come true" (Tony Robbins)

3. Next, place your written goal in a place that you can see it often for review. The review is so important because the mindset that has brought you to where you are must be totally altered in order for you to begin to see the new results you desire.

O –Open your mind to its endless possibilities:

"Whatever we plant in our subconscious mind and nourish with repetition and emotion, will one day become a reality" – EARL NIGHTINGALE

Goodnews: you can improve your credit!

The mind, our thought power; is the greatest but most unused power in the whole Universe. To achieve your dream, you must realise and use this great power. Your mind is divided into the conscious and the subconscious parts. The conscious mind is only 10% powerful and it is the part with which we think, plan, analyse and rationalise. The subconscious mind on the other hand, is where the real power lies; as it is what creates, controls, and determines our outcomes. The subconscious is the long term memory, the realm of emotions and feelings, habit formation and patterns, addiction, creativity, spiritual connections and intuition.

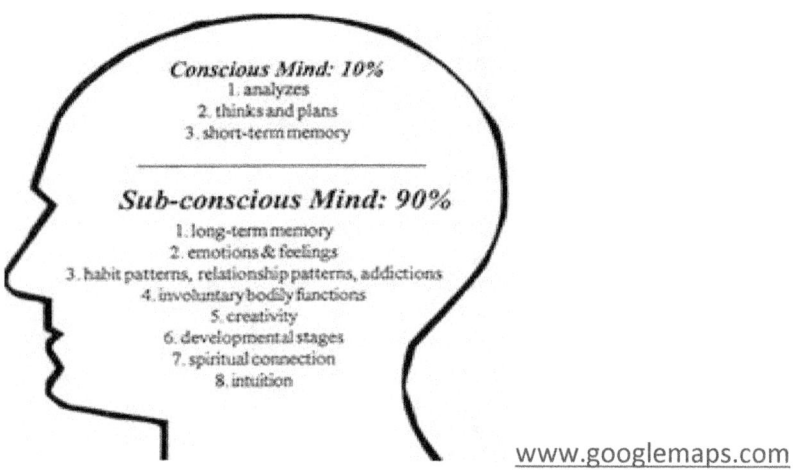

www.googlemaps.com

It is your subconscious mind that determines your result. It cannot choose the result you desire, you have to do that with your conscious mind, but once that desire reaches the

Goodnews: you can improve your credit!

subconscious mind, it must manifest because the subconscious cannot say "*no*" to the images that reaches it, it MUST bring them into reality.

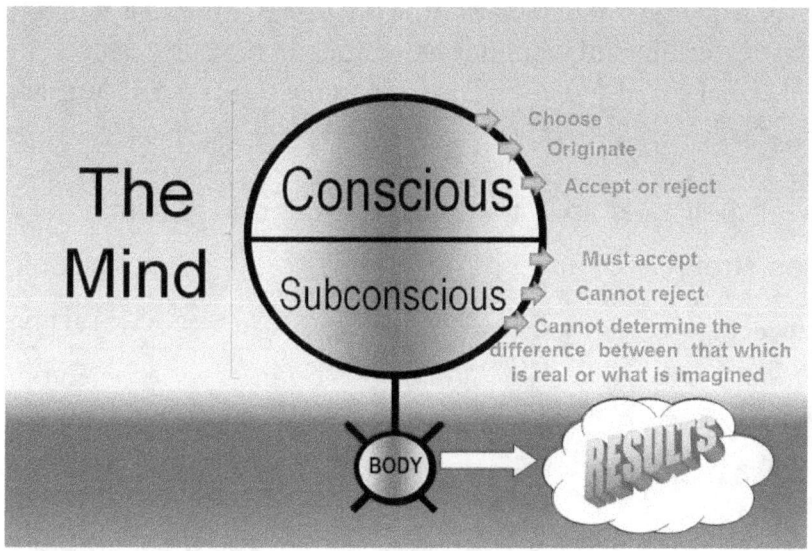

www.googlemaps.com

So as you read through your written goals and review them, you reaffirm your determination to achieve your set goals, this way, you strengthen this image of your desire on your conscious mind. When it gets strong enough, it will automatically pass unto your subconscious. Once your subconscious receives it, it will get to work immediately and will not stop until it brings that desire to fruition.

Goodnews: you can improve your credit!

C Create a vision Board

"Create a vision and never let the environment, other people's beliefs, or the limits of what has been done in the past shape your decisions." – **TONY ROBBINS**

To successfully hold your image in your conscious mind until it becomes strong enough to be passed unto the subconscious;  you need a vision board. Every successful person on Earth strongly agrees that you must create a *physical* vision board to realise your goals. As Jack Canfield puts it; "your vision board is the most powerful tool available to you for realising your goals. This powerful tool serves as your image of the future - a tangible representation of where you are going. It represents your dreams, your goals, and your ideal life". A vision board should essentially contain these:

✓ Pictures of the goal that you wish to achieve

Goodnews: you can improve your credit!

- ✓ Images or pictures which represent the feelings and emotions that you want to attract into your life

- ✓ Words which explain the status you wish to achieve. Ensure you write these in the affirmative

- ✓ A picture of yourself; if you like but please make sure that it is a picture of you in a very happy mood. One that you will always like to look at and that makes you proud of yourself. If your goal is to change your appearance, say loose a couple of pounds then put a picture of yourself before you put on the extra weight on.

Goodnews: you can improve your credit!

✓ Specifically, for the purpose of repairing your credit, you would want to write on your vision board the credit score that you wish to attain in the time frame that you have chosen.

When you're done, make sure you place this in a place where you'll be able to see it many times each day.

Goodnews: you can improve your credit!

Goal-cards: pocket-size vision boards

You will need to carry your vision board with you wherever you go and to successfully do that you need your goal-cards. My personal definition of a goal card is "pocket-size vision board". A goal card should be your written target to be accomplished in a specified period of time. You will not be able to pursue all of the goals on your vision board at once, so you must divide them into "bite size" forms. That is, the particular goal that you wish to achieve within a 30 day period for example. It should be written on a goal card. Then you must carry this goal card in your purse or wallet or pocket, every day, everywhere.

> Goal Card
> **By the 31st of December, 2017; I will have in my possession the sum of £100,000.**

The good thing about this is that you can pull it out to read several times during the day, especially if you do not work from home. This way, even though you are not seeing your entire vision board, you can look at, meditate upon and re-affirm your goal several times in a day.

Goodnews: you can improve your credit!

An example of a goal card would read thus: by the 31st of December, 2017 I will achieve a credit score of 550 out of 700". When you begin reading your goal to yourself, it would sound so impossible. Don't be surprised, it might be because all along, you have developed a negative self-image about yourself which has controlled and determined your outcome up until this point, so trying to say positive things about yourself would conflict with that established self-image. But do not despair, do not give in to those negative thoughts; just continue to repeat your desired outcome to yourself.

Be careful not to read it to the hearing of people because their reaction or scorn and laughter, may discourage you. So read out your goal card to yourself privately. Bob Proctor says in his book, *you were born rich,* that research has shown that you can change your self-image within 90 days, by looking at and reaffirming the new outcome that you desire. Remember "words are containers of power, you choose what kind of power they carry" –Joyce Meyer

Goodnews: you can improve your credit!

U- Unleash your potential within

> You cannot afford to live in potential for the rest of your life, at some point you have to unleash the potential, and make your move. -Eric Thomas

Everyone has enormous potential lying dormant within them; only those who unleash their own succeed. As a science teacher, *dormancy*; is one phenomenon that has intrigued me for years. We use that word to describe the state of inactivity, despite great ability within. For example, plants which lose all their leaves in the winter months are said to go into a period of dormancy. So are animals which sleep through the winter months. Then more fascinating are seeds, which when dried and stored away, and can stay in that state of dormancy for several thousands of years; just as a seed!

In each of the above referred cases, the period of inactivity ends as soon as conditions return to normal, and these organisms break out of their near-death-state; and blossom into a lively, active, productive state. Imagine how a seemingly lifeless acorn seed can become a massive oak tree if given the right conditions. Meaning that that huge tree was hidden away in that lifeless seed all along!

Goodnews: you can improve your credit!

In the same way, you have within you massive abilities to become whatever you desire to become. But until you unleash that potential within, you're just like the dormant acorn seed.

Therefore, I charge you today to take hold of the great conditions presented to you on this course, decide once and for all that you will no longer lie *dormant* like the acorn seed but rather, you will unleash the great potential within you and grow into that huge oak tree that you were created to be. Unleash that power within you, today!

S-success is inevitable

Success is the progressive realization of worthwhile dreams and goals (Earl Nightingale).

The S in 'focus' sums up the destination that you are sure to arrive at as you put into practice all the other 4 letters before it, and that is 'success'. As Earl Nightingale puts it, success is a progressive realisation of a worthy Ideal. The truly successful person is one, who takes little steps, daily; towards his/her goal.

As some wise teachers have truly explained, it is not the absence of failure but the ability to keep on going despite the failures encountered that defines a person.

So as you have decided to go through; or have gone through with this course in a bid to repair/improve your bad credit status, the outcome that awaits you is success. You will definitely gain your financial freedom within the time frame you have set for yourself.

Finally, let me state here that without doubt, I am convinced that the principles and guidelines outlined on this course have served the very purpose for which they were intended. But even better, is the fact that these same principles and guidelines can literally be applied to other areas of human endeavours where challenges need to be overcome, be they physical, emotional, spiritual, social, marital or economical; with the same positive outcomes, guaranteed. These tried and tested "success principles wear no work-clothes except the ones you put on them; yourself". In a short sentence, these success principles would accomplish whatever task you set out to achieve with them.

Thank you.

ivycrowncredit@gmail.com
Goodnews: you can improve your credit!

REFERENCE Page

– http://www.investopedia.com/terms/f/ficoscore.asp

- http://www.experian.co.uk/consumer/faq/CCJ2.html   Accessed March 12 2016

- www.experia.co.uk

-http://jackcanfield.com/how-to-create-an-empowering-vision-book/#sthash.d716oV0s.dpuf

- http://jackcanfield.com/how-to-create-an-empowering-vision-book/

-http://www.mindtraininginstitute.net/photo-gallery/vision-boards.html

Goodnews: you can improve your credit!

www.ingramcontent.com/pod-product-compliance
Lightning Source LLC
Chambersburg PA
CBHW070318230526
45470CB00002B/936